Microscopic Life
in your
Body

BRIAN WARD

Contents and definitions

Bacteria

Bacteria are tiny organisms that are far too small to be seen without a microscope. They may be rounded, threadlike, or rod-shaped, and some of them can creep around, using waving threads called **flagella**. Some bacteria need **oxygen** to live, while others are killed by the oxygen in the air.

Viruses

Viruses are even tinier than bacteria. Unlike many bacteria, viruses need to infect a living cell if they are to grow and reproduce. They take over the whole of the workings of the cell and turn it into a virus factory. This usually kills the cell as the new viruses are released.

Fungi

A **fungus** is a small organism that mostly feeds on dead and **decaying** material. Some small fungi called "yeasts" can cause disease when they grow on moist parts of the body surface, such as between the toes.

Tiny animals

Tiny animal-like creatures called **Protista** cause serious diseases such as **malaria** in some tropical parts of the world.

Mites and lice

Large numbers of tiny spider-like creatures called **mites** live on the human body and in beds, feeding on small pieces of skin. Other mites burrow into human skin. Small, flat insects called **lice** can live on the skin, feeding on blood.

Living with microbes

People cannot get away from microbes. With every breath taken, millions of them are inhaled.

How do microbes get inside people?

Microbes are microscopic living things. Most of these tiny organisms that are breathed in are breathed out again. Those that stay in are quickly attacked by the body, so they hardly do any harm. Millions of bugs are also swallowed with every mouthful of food or drink, although most of these are killed by the strong acid in the stomach. Everything touched is covered with bacteria, which are transferred (usually without doing any harm) from the fingers to the mouth when people eat.

◄

Each mouthful of food is loaded with bacteria and viruses.

TRY IT YOURSELF

How big are cells?
Put some sticky tape on your wrist. Rip it off quickly and place it under a microscope. You should be able to see some dead skin cells on it.

Friendly microbes

Millions of harmless bacteria live on the surface of human skin, but most of the "good" bacteria live in the intestines, where they help to keep a person healthy. Most microbes can live on and in people without causing any harm at all. In fact, at least 95 percent of them are harmless. People need some microbes to stay healthy. Disease is caused only when the microbes grow and increase in numbers faster than the body can kill them.

MICRO FACTS

The microbe farm

The human body is made up of millions and millions of cells—but for every one body cell there are 19 bacteria cells. In addition, there are many viruses lurking inside body cells, and other organisms living on skin. The body is a tremendous microbe farm!

▼ *The human intestines are home to millions of bacteria that help the body digest food.*

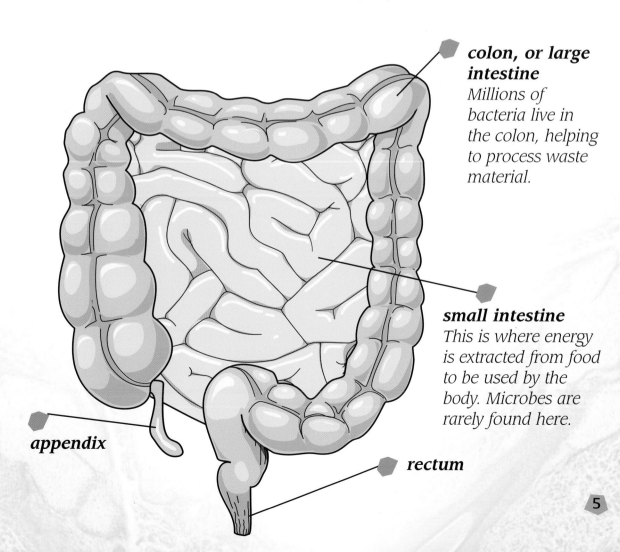

colon, or large intestine
Millions of bacteria live in the colon, helping to process waste material.

small intestine
This is where energy is extracted from food to be used by the body. Microbes are rarely found here.

appendix

rectum

"Good" microbes

The microbes that live in the colon are "good" microbes because they help to break down food.

How do bacteria help with digestion?

Food is digested in the intestines. It is broken down by substances called "enzymes" so it can be absorbed and used by the body. Some food cannot be digested in this way. The bacteria in the colon help to break down these indigestible food parts so the body can use it properly. The bacteria use some of the food for themselves, but they also make other useful food substances that can be used. Some vitamins are produced in the colon by "good" bacteria.

Eating bacteria

Many of these "good" bacteria are like those that grow in milk and make it sour. Some people like to eat "live" yogurt (which contains huge numbers of these bacteria) to add to the numbers in their colon.

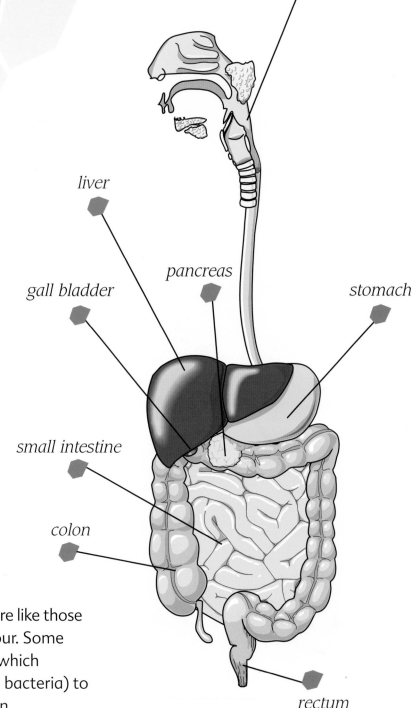

food pipe

liver

pancreas

gall bladder

stomach

small intestine

colon

rectum

6

Some amazing facts about the bacteria in humans

- Humans have about two and a quarter pounds (1 kg) of bacteria in the colon.
- A quarter ounce (7 g) of **feces** contains 700,000 million bacteria.
- Every day, people on Earth produce more than two and a quarter billion pounds (5 billion kg) of feces. That's a lot of bacteria!

Smelly microbes . . .

One sign of the "good" bacteria in the colon is farting! The bacteria working away in the colon produce gas that escapes from the body as a belch or fart. Most people fart 10 to 15 times each day. Even this is nothing compared to cows, who fart so much of a gas called "methane" that some scientists think they may be helping to make the whole surface of the planet heat up.

. . . and skinny microbes

"Good," or harmless, microbes also live in huge numbers on the skin, feeding on the oily **sebum** produced from the tiny pits, or **follicles**, where hairs grow. Their great numbers crowd out harmful bacteria so they cannot grow and cause skin diseases.

TRY IT YOURSELF

How hairy are you?

Use a hand magnifier to study your own skin. How many hair follicles do you see on the back of your hand? Ask a friend if you can study his/her face. Imagine all the "good" bacteria living in the follicles you can see.

The immune system

If people are surrounded by billions of germs waiting to feed on their bodies, why aren't they ill all the time?

Germs have markers called "antigens" on their surface. Each lymphocyte recognizes a particular antigen, like a key fits a lock.

bacterium

antigen (or marker)

lymphocytes

lymphocyte locks onto a marker

lymphocyte multiplies rapidly

memory cell (remembers invader's antigens)

When the lymphocyte recognizes a germ, it divides to produce two types of cells: memory cells that memorize the antigen, and plasma cells that release **antibodies**. *Antibodies disable the germ.*

antibody

plasma cell (produces antibodies)

◆ Identifying the enemy

Threatened every day by billions of germs, the body has a very good defense: the immune system. Huge numbers of special white blood cells, called **lymphocytes**, are carried around the body in the blood, ready to find an invading microbe germ. As soon as lymphocytes touch an unfamiliar cell or substance, they begin to produce chemicals called "antibodies," which attack the invaders, killing or damaging them. The lymphocytes also make memory cells, so the body recognizes the germ in the future. The cells then "learn" how to make a new antibody, which over a few days builds up **immunity** to overcome the invading microbes.

⬡ Resisting infection

Once they have made an antibody that will kill a particular microbe, the lymphocytes remember how to do it. If the same microbe enters the body some time later, they respond by producing the proper antibody very quickly, so the infection never has the chance to develop properly. This is called "immunity." Humans catch most diseases only once, because after that, they are fully immune. However, people may still have lots of colds, because colds can be caused by hundreds of different types of viruses, which all cause similar coughs and sneezes. A person would have to become immune to all of them to prevent all colds.

Coughs and sneezes do spread diseases, ▶
so covering the mouth can reduce the
risk of infecting other people.

MICRO FACTS
Virus in disguise

The flu, or influenza, virus, which is very different from the cold virus, often causes epidemics (when lots of people become ill). The virus changes slightly each year, so even if a person has had the disease before, the body may not recognize the slightly altered virus and will not be able to make an antibody right away. The flu virus is very strange because it seems to live naturally in ducks and pigs in China, and a different type of flu spreads from them to humans every few years.

Bigger creatures

There are lots of tiny creatures with legs walking around on people's skin all the time. Most of these are harmless.

Creatures in human skin

Humans carry around tiny creatures called "mites," which are smaller than a grain of salt. They live in the pores and hair follicles in the face, and especially in the roots of the eyelashes. These little creatures feed on oil and dead skin cells, and though they look nasty, they are quite harmless.

Mites living in the pores of your face are only 16 one-thousandths of an inch (0.4 mm) long.

MICRO FACTS

Burrowing mites

One type of mite can cause unpleasant skin infections, burrowing through the skin and causing itchy red tracks. This condition is called **scabies**, and it sometimes affects people who do not take care to clean themselves properly. Scabies is spread by touching an infected person, or sometimes by touching a pet suffering from a skin condition called "mange."

Mites in the bed

Some other types of mites, called "dust mites," walk around on the skin, feeding on loose flakes of dead skin. These mites are too small to see, but there can be millions of them in a bed or pillow, feeding on bits of shed skin. Many more of them live in the carpet. Mites are related to spiders, but they have much shorter legs. These mites are harmless, although their droppings make some people sneeze or wheeze. This is a common allergy, and people who suffer from it use special pillows and mattress covers.

▲ *A bed may contain millions of microscopic mites, feeding on bits of shed skin.*

What is a nit?

Lice also live on skin, in the hair, where they feed on blood. They are small, flat insects that are difficult to see as they cling to a hair. Young lice are completely transparent. As they grow, they become the color of the hair they live in. Usually they are identified only when their egg sacs, called **nits**, are seen in the hair. Nits look like tiny grains of yellowish rice. Lice and nits are spread by contact with an infected person, and the condition is very common among groups of children who play together. The best way to get rid of lice and their nits is to comb a special chemical through the hair with a fine-toothed comb.

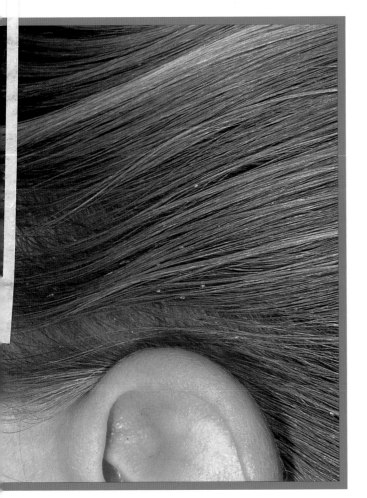

◄ *Nits are the egg sacs of mites, which live in the hair and suck blood.*

Spreading diseases

Microbes are very resourceful and can get into people's bodies in several different ways.

Breathing in

The most common way to become infected is by breathing in the air after someone coughs or sneezes. Coughing and sneezing expel millions of bacteria or viruses from people's lungs. Colds and the flu are the most common infections spread in this way. Hundreds of different viruses can cause the symptoms of a cold.

◄

Every time a person sneezes, a stream of infected water drops are shot across the room.

A sneeze spreads disease

A sneeze can blast a stream of water droplets about 27 inches (2 m), and if a person has a cold, each tiny droplet may contain millions of microbes ready to be breathed in by someone else. This is why it is healthful as well as polite to put a hand over the mouth when coughing or sneezing.

TRY IT YOURSELF

Measure 27 inches (2 m) from your mouth to see how far your sneeze can travel!

🔹 Microbes in the mouth

More than 500 different types of bacteria live in the human mouth! Most are harmless, but they can be transferred between people by kissing, sharing a toothbrush, or drinking from an unwashed glass or cup. Cold sores are also spread by this sort of contact, and so is a virus infection called "glandular fever," which often affects older children and students.

🔹 People can be catching!

Many people become infectious before they show any signs of illness, which is why childhood diseases such as mumps and chickenpox spread so quickly through groups of children.

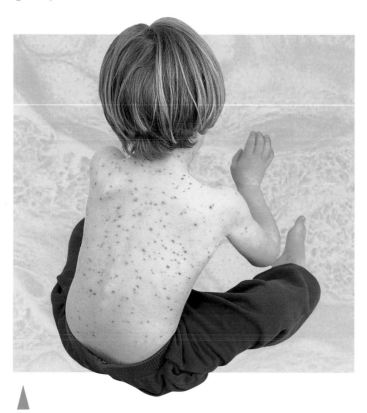

Spots and rashes like this mean that someone is infected with viruses or bacteria.

MICRO FACTS

Pet threat

Believe it or not, more than 100 types of microbes can be spread by the saliva in the mouths of cats and dogs. Never let pets lick your face or share your food, as this will leave lots of bacteria around your mouth. *Salmonella* bacteria are often found in pet birds and especially in reptiles. They are also found in uncooked eggs and chicken meat. The animals are not usually affected by the bacteria, but they can cause very unpleasant stomach upsets when they get into humans. Hands should be washed carefully after handling animals, and food should be cooked thoroughly to kill any bacteria.

An upset stomach

Why is it that when people travel to a new place on vacation they may get diarrhea?

People can have intestinal troubles on vacation. ▼

🛡 Traveler's tummy

People have billions of bacteria living in their intestines, and over the years the body gets used to them. The different types of microbes all live together, helping to digest food. But in unfamiliar places, food or drinking water may contain different microbes that live in the local people. This happens when feces are not treated properly in a sewage system, so the microbes they contain pass into the drinking water, and then into another person's body. Once the new type of bacteria enter the digestive system from food or drink, they begin to grow, upsetting the balance of the bacteria already there. This is what causes **diarrhea** and stomach pains, and it can take a few days before a person's own bacteria overcome the new ones.

Mucky food

Even worse stomach upsets can be caused if food is not treated in a healthful way or cooked thoroughly, giving the dangerous bacteria the chance to multiply. This can happen if someone handling food has poor **hygiene** (not washing their hands properly after using the toilet). Flies carry infection, too, on their feet. If they walk on food, they spread bacteria, so care must be taken to cover food that is left in the open.

Flies walking on food often ▶
spread bacteria and viruses
that cause diarrhea.

MICRO FACTS

What is food poisoning?

Food poisoning happens when food has not been handled hygienically, enabling bacteria to grow and sometimes produce poisons called **toxins**. Common foods such as chicken and eggs often cause a form of food poisoning called salmonellosis, which can make people very ill. Another very dangerous form of food poisoning is caused by bacteria related to the ones living in the human intestines, called *E. coli*, which can lead to serious disease outbreaks.

Bacterial attack

Usually it takes a large number of bacteria to start an infection that will make people ill. Ordinarily, the body can overcome small numbers of bacteria very quickly, but if bacteria get into the body in huge numbers, they may cause serious harm.

Where do bacteria live?

Most bacteria live and grow in their favorite part of the body. *Streptococci* bacteria are a common cause of sore throats and **tonsillitis**. They live in the tissues, feeding on them and the liquid around the cells, and as they grow and divide, they produce poisonous waste materials called "toxins." These poisons are carried around the body in the blood, causing a hot and achy feeling.

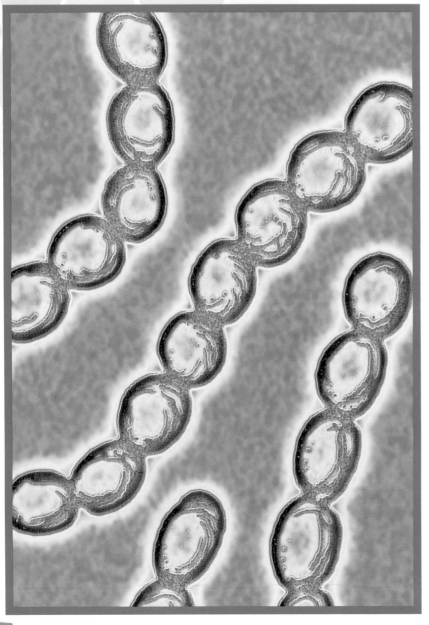

◀ *The* Streptococci *bacteria that often cause sore throats may grow in long chains.*

Meningitis

Meningitis is a very serious disease that can be caused by bacteria infecting the skin-like covering of the brain, where it causes a very bad headache and a high temperature. Other types of meningitis are caused by viruses.

Have I caught something?

After having been exposed to an infection, people do not become ill immediately, if at all. The period of time between catching an infection and becoming ill is called the "incubation period." Usually, more than two weeks can pass after becoming infected before signs of the illness appear:

Chickenpox	14-16 days
Mumps	14-24 days
Rubella (German measles)	14-21 days

How long will I be ill?

Some infections are acute. This means that they come on suddenly and clear up quite quickly. Most sore throats are infections of this type. A "chronic" infection lasts much longer. One example of a chronic infection is the disease **tuberculosis (TB)**. The TB bacteria are breathed into the lungs and often remain there for years without changing very much. Then they can suddenly start growing again and cause very serious problems.

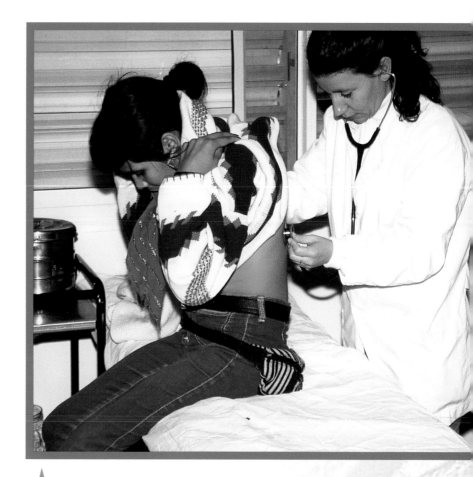

▲ *A doctor uses a stethoscope to hear the wheezing in the lungs caused by infection.*

Tooth attack

The mouth is warm and wet. This **habitat** provides the ideal conditions for bacteria to grow. Some mouth bacteria cause tooth decay and cavities (holes), and may even cause the loss of a tooth.

Bacteria in the mouth

Most of the bacteria in the mouth cause no problems, but there is one type called *Streptococcus mutans* ("Strep" for short) that causes tooth decay. Strep bacteria are tiny round organisms that feed on the sugar in food and produce a waste material called **lactic acid**. This acid eats into the hard **enamel** surface of the tooth, softening it and causing a cavity that lets other dangerous bacteria get inside and do more damage. Drinking soft drinks often makes the damage worse, because they also contain acid.

*Bacteria in **plaque** attack a tooth that has had its enamel damaged by acid.* ▼

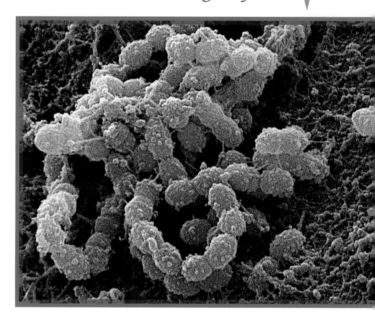

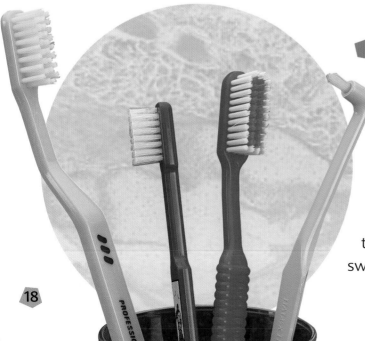

The threat from sugar

When people eat sweets, the sugar is just what the Strep bacteria need to grow and cause damage. They form a slimy layer of bacteria over the teeth, called "plaque." This can be felt with the tongue after eating sweet foods, and it needs to be removed quickly by brushing the teeth thoroughly. People who do not eat sweet things have 90 percent fewer cavities!

🔷 Losing teeth

As well as causing cavities, a layer of plaque on the teeth can do lots more damage if it is not removed properly. It gradually hardens into a stony brown layer around the bottom of the tooth, and this makes the gums sore. Then more harmful bacteria get into the base of the tooth and may cause so much damage that eventually the tooth has to be taken out.

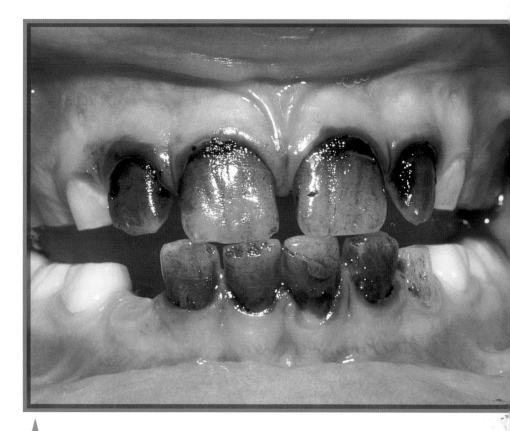

Bacteria and the plaque they cause can damage teeth so much that they eventually have to be removed.

See how acid attacks teeth!

If you have a tooth that the tooth fairy forgot to take away, drop it into a clear plastic bottle containing a soft drink (check the label to see that the drink contains phosphoric or **citric acid**). If you cannot find a tooth, use a piece of chicken bone, which is similar to tooth enamel. Stand it in a safe place. Then, after a couple weeks, check to see what has happened to the tooth or piece of bone. Think about what could be happening in your own mouth! When you have finished with it, throw everything away carefully.

Virus attack

Viruses cause most of the common illnesses of children. Mumps, rubella, and chickenpox are all caused by virus infections. They are all highly contagious, causing outbreaks of disease that affect large groups of children.

Virus takeover

Viruses have a peculiar way of life. Some experts even think that they are not alive at all because they cannot grow or reproduce on their own—to do so they have to enter the cells of a living organism that can. When viruses enter the body, they are normally attacked by the immune system, but if some of them escape, they can get into body cells. Each body cell contains a command center called the "nucleus," which gives instructions to the cell about what it should do. The virus enters this nucleus and takes over, giving its own instructions to make huge numbers of new viruses. Eventually these tiny particles burst out of the cell and float away to infect other healthy cells.

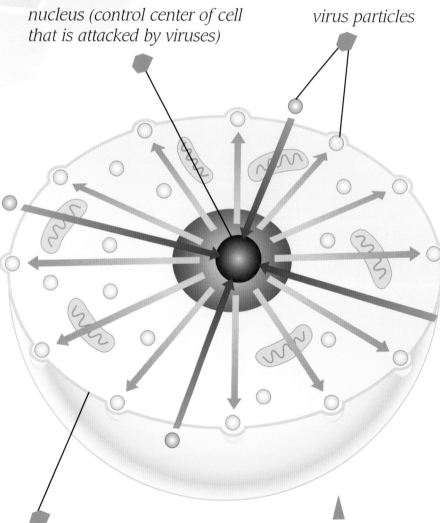

nucleus (control center of cell that is attacked by viruses)

virus particles

cell membrane

A diagram of a cell being attacked by a virus. The virus particles multiply quickly in the nucleus and then bud off from the cell wall to infect other cells.

Sneaky viruses

While these viruses are in the cell, the body's defenses cannot find them. The viruses are attacked only when they burst out. It is the waste materials, or poisons, that are released when the viruses burst out from cells that cause the typical aching feeling associated with a cold or other virus infection. Illnesses caused by viruses are usually "acute" infections that clear up quite quickly. However, they may leave sufferers feeling very wobbly for a while, and they are likely to catch some other infection while they are weakened.

Tiny flu virus particles are budded off from the surface of an infected cell to spread the infection to other cells. ▼

What causes AIDS?

HIV is the virus associated with the serious disease **AIDS**. It is very unusual because it infects and damages the cells of the immune system that normally fight infections, so the body has no effective way to defend itself. HIV is also unusual because it takes a long time after infection for its effects to appear. The virus itself does not necessarily lead to AIDS, but lots of infections that would normally be prevented by the immune system are able to cause immense damage.

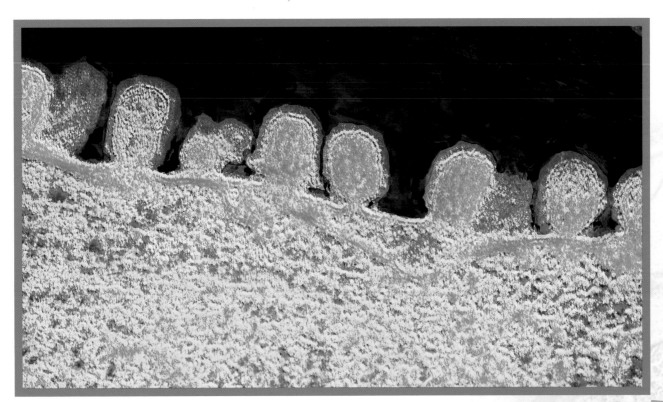

Skin microbes

People are often aware when microbes infect their skin and cause disease because they can see the spots and pimples that they produce.

What causes pimples?

Large numbers of bacteria live in the hair follicles on the skin. The oily substance called "sebum" (produced in the root of hairs) is an ideal food for them. If the follicle becomes blocked, the oily sebum collects, and the trapped bacteria multiply, causing a red spot or pimple. Sometimes the bacteria move deeper into the skin and attack the tissues, causing a boil. The yellowish **pus** in a boil is the remains of dead bacteria and the body cells attacking them.

Oily sebum trapped in skin follicles encourages the growth of bacteria that cause spots and pimples.

Cold sores

Viruses often attack the skin around the lips, causing painful cold sores. Once a person has been infected with the cold sore virus, it will get inside the cells, where it stays until he/she is weakened by tiredness or some other infection. Then it breaks out and produces cold sores, which usually come back when a person feels tired and worn out.

Foot fungus

Athlete's Foot is an infection caused by a tiny fungus that feeds on skin cells, usually between the toes. The skin becomes sore and peels, and sometimes even toe nails become infected. Athlete's Foot is often caught at swimming pools, as it can easily survive in the warm, wet habitat. The infection can be treated with over-the-counter medicines.

Tiny threads of fungus cause Athlete's Foot. They can also cause skin infections in other parts of the body.

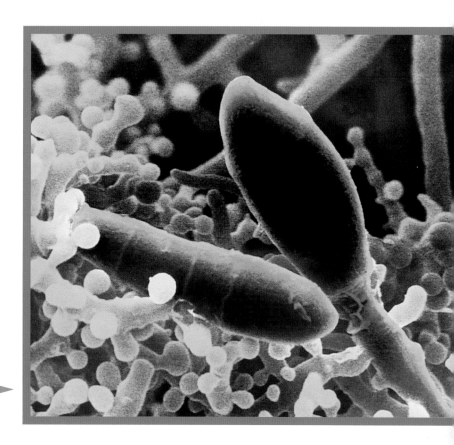

Warts and verrucae

Warts are caused by a virus. The cells it infects divide and grow, producing a lump on the skin, usually on the hands. Another form of wart, called a **verruca**, grows on the sole of the foot, but the lump grows inward, so it is uncomfortable to walk on it. The verruca virus, like Athlete's Foot, thrives in swimming pools and locker rooms.

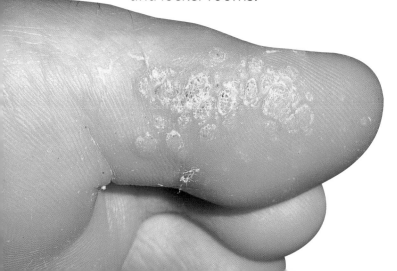

MICRO FACTS

What's in a wart?
The outer layer of the skin is made of lots of cells that divide very quickly. The skin cells on the surface die and flake off as new cells grow beneath them. The wart virus infects these dividing cells and makes them divide even more quickly. They build up into a lump, or wart, because they grow faster than they die off.

Hot bugs

Microbes can cause very serious diseases in tropical parts of the world—and sometimes in other countries, too. These microbes are known as "hot bugs."

Burying victims of the "Black Death"— a medieval "hot bug" plague.

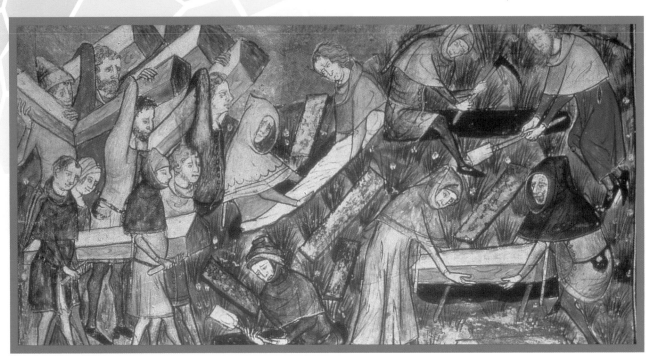

MICRO FACTS The Black Death

Around 600 years ago, one in every three people in Europe was killed by the Black Death, or bubonic plague. This was a disease of rats caused by bacteria. People were infected in two ways: firstly, **fleas** would bite the rats and pick up the bacteria. Then the fleas would bite people, transferring the bacteria from the rats to the people. Secondly, the disease spread through the air

when infected people coughed up the bacteria from their lungs. This bacteria would then be breathed in by other people, infecting them. In those days people did not know about microorganisms or how they spread disease. The plague moved across Europe in waves, but it gradually became less serious. Now it very rarely causes disease and can be treated with **antibiotics** (see page 29).

Killing off the virus

Smallpox was a killer disease that existed for thousands of years. It is a virus that causes masses of sores over the skin; it killed many of the people that it infected. Smallpox is the only human disease that has ever been wiped out in nature, due to **vaccination** (see page 28) of all the people living in the areas where it existed. Some of the virus is still kept in laboratories.

*These tiny yellow ▶ microbes are malaria **parasites** entering red blood cells. The cells die, making the infected person very ill.*

Mosquito threat

Malaria is a common disease in tropical countries that is spread by the bite of an infected mosquito. It is caused by tiny microbes called *Plasmodium,* which are neither bacteria nor viruses. They belong to a separate group of microbes called "Protista." Malaria causes very high temperatures and affects millions of people living in the tropics. Many children in Africa are killed by this disease.

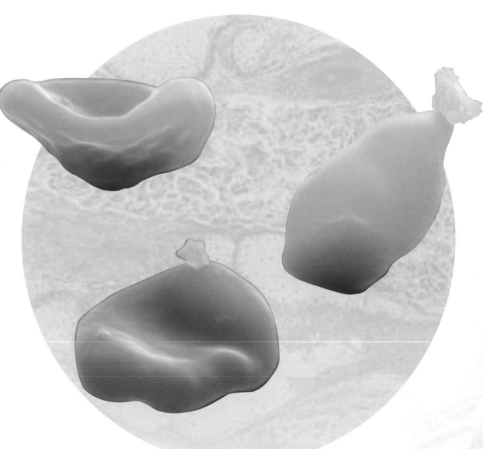

New threats

Many of the most dangerous tropical diseases are animal infections that can also attack people. Some of these diseases cause outbreaks when people come into contact with the animals as they move into new living areas. **Ebola** fever is one such killer disease, caused by a virus. It attacks people in the jungles of parts of Africa, and it is even killing off gorilla populations. HIV (the virus causing the condition called "AIDS") is also thought to have arisen in Africa, probably in apes or monkeys, but it has now spread around the world. It can be caught only by contact with the body fluids, such as blood, of an infected person.

Keeping clean

There are lots of ways to avoid infection with microbes, and also to prevent passing them on to other people.

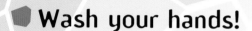

Wash your hands!

Washing hands after using the toilet and before eating is the most important single thing a person can do to avoid becoming infected by the microbes that are all around. Rinsing the hands is not enough—they need a good scrubbing with soap and water. It's important to clean under the nails, where dirt and microbes can gather. People must also clean themselves properly after using the toilet.

Hands should be scrubbed after using the toilet and before touching food.

People must be sure to wash their hands thoroughly after changing a baby's diaper, touching trash, cleaning a pet's litter box, handling raw meat, or playing with animals. All of these activities can be the cause of infection.

Today, many soaps have an antibacterial agent added.

Skin care

Showering and bathing help keep the body clean by reducing the numbers of bacteria on the surface of the skin. Frequent and thorough washing with soap will help keep skin clear of spots, too, though sometimes these cannot be avoided, especially in teenagers. Disinfectants or medicated soaps should not be used on the face. These will remove too much of the skin's natural protective oils—and the harmless bacteria that crowd out the ones causing the spots.

▲ *Sebum soon makes hair look greasy and straggly if it is not washed away regularly.*

MICRO FACTS

Smelly feet!

Smelly feet and armpits are caused by bacteria feeding on the oily sebum in hair follicles. Frequent washing removes the sebum, so the bacteria have nothing to feed on, and then there's no sweaty smell. Socks and sneakers smell bad for just the same reason. They should be washed often!

Fighting back

Bodies can usually fight infection, but sometimes they need some help. People can do this by encouraging the body to strengthen its defenses, or by taking drugs to kill harmful bacteria.

🔶 What is vaccination?

One way to prevent disease caused by bacteria or viruses is to kill them as soon as they enter the body. A body can be encouraged to fight back quickly by a process called vaccination. Vaccines are usually injected, or sometimes swallowed (like the polio vaccine children are given), before a person is exposed to infections. The vaccines contain weak or harmless microbes, dead microbes, or sometimes, just some important parts of the microbes. The body's immune system recognizes the "invaders" and reacts as though they were a real threat to health, producing protective antibodies. When the real invaders strike, the antibodies can then be produced very quickly, preventing an infection from developing. Vaccination is valuable because it works to protect against both bacteria and virus attack.

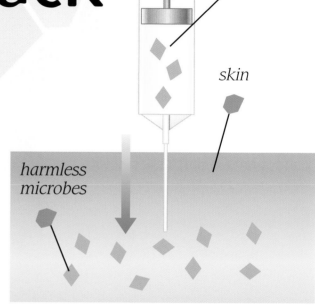

vaccine

skin

harmless microbes

1. A person is injected with harmless microbes or bits of microbes that do not cause the disease.

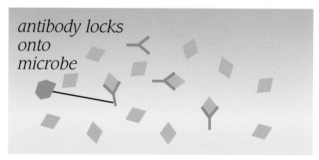

antibody locks onto microbe

2. Although the microbial material is harmless, the body still recognizes it and makes antibodies against it.

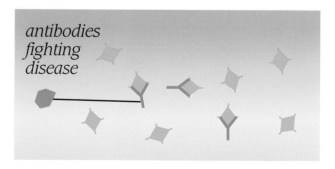

antibodies fighting disease

3. If the body is invaded by the real microbes, the immune system responds immediately with huge numbers of antibodies to destroy the disease.

Did you know?

In 1798, Edward Jenner infected a boy with cowpox, a harmless cattle disease so similar to the killer disease smallpox that it made the boy completely immune. But Jenner still did not know what caused disease. In 1885, Louis Pasteur was the first person to prove that microbes caused infections and to develop vaccines to provide protection.

Antibiotics to kill bacteria

Some natural substances fight bacteria (but not viruses) by interfering with the way that they reproduce. These substances are called "antibiotics." They weaken the bacteria, which are then quickly killed by the body's own defenses. Antibiotics can treat an infection only once it has appeared, so, unlike vaccines, they cannot be used to prevent infection. They do not kill viruses, so they do not help treat a cold or the flu.

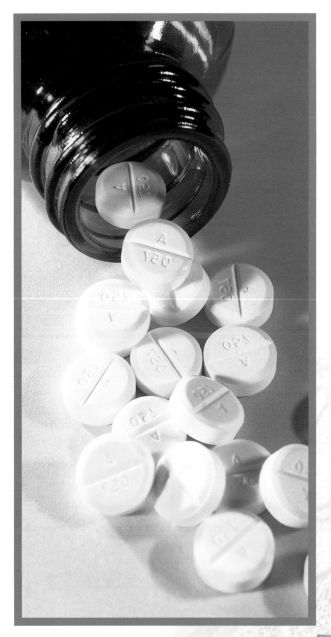

MICRO FACTS

Can antibiotics make people feel worse?

People who have been ill and taken antibiotics know how well they can work, but the drugs may also cause diarrhea. This is because the antibiotics kill off the "good" microbes that live in the body as well as the ones causing the illness, interfering with the normal process of digestion.

Glossary

AIDS: Acquired Immune Deficiency Syndrome; a serious disease spread by contact with body fluids from an infected person.

Antibiotics: Drugs that attack bacteria and sometimes other microbes.

Antibodies: Substances produced in the body to fight invading microbes or other substances that enter the blood system.

Bacteria: Tiny single-celled microbes that live nearly everywhere, including people's bodies, food, and homes. Some bacteria can be "good," for example, by helping people digest food. Other bacteria can be "bad," because they cause diseases.

Citric acid: Sharp-tasting substance found in fruit and often added to soft drinks.

Decaying: Being broken down by microbes.

Diarrhea: Condition that may be caused by infection, in which food passes very quickly through the digestive system.

Ebola: A very dangerous, but rare, disease first found in Africa. It is caused by a virus, but no one knows how it spreads.

Enamel: The hard, shiny surface layer of the teeth.

Feces: Solid waste that remains after food is digested.

Flagella: Thin, hair-like strands found on some bacteria and other microbes. They may allow the microbe to move around.

Fleas: Tiny jumping insects, mostly found on cats, which bite and feed on blood. They also bite people.

Follicles: The tiny sockets in the skin from which hairs grow.

Fungus: Organism that breaks down dead material and sometimes also causes diseases. Most fungi are microscopic; others are large, like mushrooms.

Habitat: The place where organisms live.

HIV: Human immuno-deficiency virus; the virus that causes AIDS.

Hygiene: Measures to control the level of microbes, such as washing hands and cleaning kitchen work surfaces.

Immunity: When the body can fight off microbes, having been infected once before.

Lactic acid: Sour-tasting substance produced when bacteria cause milk to "go bad."

Lice: Tiny, flat insects that cling to hair, feeding on blood.

Lymphocytes: Body cells that fight infection.

Malaria: Tropical disease caused by tiny animal-like parasites, injected into the body by the bite of a mosquito.

Microbes: Organisms that are so small they can be seen only with the aid of a microscope.

Mites: Tiny spider-like animals that feed on skin flakes, food debris, or sometimes on people.

Nits: The cream-colored eggs of head lice.

Oxygen: Colorless gas in the air.

Parasites: Animals or other living organisms that feed on other forms of life.

Plaque: Slimy layer of bacteria covering the teeth.

Protista: Tiny animal-like organisms.

Pus: Yellowish remains of dead bacteria and body cells that fight infection.

Salmonella: Bacteria that cause the disease Salmonellosis when eaten in contaminated food.

Scabies: Itchy skin disease caused by mites that burrow under the skin surface.

Sebum: Oily liquid produced from hair follicles, helping to keep the skin flexible.

Smallpox: Very dangerous disease caused by a virus, but now extinct in nature because of vaccination programs.

Streptococci: Bad bacteria that cause fever and pain.

Tonsillitis: Painful infection of the tonsils, small fleshy patches in the back of the throat.

Toxins: Poisonous substances produced by some types of bacteria.

Tuberculosis (TB): A serious lung disease caused by bacteria; it can be prevented by vaccination.

Vaccination: Process that produces immunity to an infection. Vaccines may be taken by mouth or injected. They contain dead or harmless microbes, or parts of them, and they cause the body to react by producing antibodies.

Verruca: Virus infection of the skin on the sole of the foot.

Viruses: Very simple organisms that can grow and reproduce only inside living cells. All viruses are parasites.

Warts: Virus infections of the skin, producing small lumps.

Further information

The following web sites contain lots of useful information about microbes and their effects on the body:

AIDS Handbook: An Introduction: **http://www.eastchester.k12. ny.us/schools/ms/AIDS/AIDS1. html**

Bacterial Growth and Multiplication: **http://www.cellsalive.com/ ecoli.htm**

Eyelash Mites: **http://geocities. com/thesciencefiles/eyelash/ creatures.html**

How Lou Got the Flu: **http://www.amnh.org/national center/infection/04_lou/04_lou. html**

Learning About Allergies: **http://kidshealth.org/kid/health _problems/allergy/allergies.html**

Microbes—Invisible Invaders, Amazing Allies: **http://www. miamisci.org/microbes/ facts18.html**

Microbes in Sickness and in Health: **http://www.niaid. nih.gov/publications/ microbes.htm**

Scabies: **http://www.aad. org/pamphlets/Scabies.html**

Stalking the Mysterious Microbe: **http://www.microbe.org**

index

First published in 2003 by Franklin Watts
96 Leonard Street, London EC2A 4XD

Franklin Watts Australia
45—51 Huntley Street, Alexandria
NSW 2015

This edition published under license from
Franklin Watts. All rights reserved.
Copyright © 2003 Franklin Watts

Published in the United States by
Smart Apple Media
1980 Lookout Drive, North Mankato,
Minnesota 56003

U.S. publication copyright © 2005 Smart
Apple Media. International copyright
reserved in all countries. No part of this book
may be reproduced in any form without
written permission from the publisher.

Library of Congress Cataloging-in-Publication
Data

Ward, Brian R.
Microscopic life in your body / Brian Ward.
p. c.m. — (Micro World)
Includes index.
Summary: Describes different kinds of
microbes, both beneficial and harmful, that
are found in the human body.
ISBN 1-58340-470-8
1. Body, Human—Microbiology—Juvenile
literature. [1. Body, Human. 2.
Microorganisms.] I. Title.

QR171.A1W37 2004
612—dc22   2003058962

Editor: Kate Banham
Designer: Joelle Wheelwright
Art direction: Peter Scoulding
Illustrations: David Graham
Picture research: Diana Morris
Educational consultant: Dot Jackson

The publishers would like to thank the following for
permission to reproduce photographs in this book:
Anthony Bannister/Corbis: 15t.
Mark Clarke/SPL: 13b. CNRI/SPL: 2b, 21.
A.Crump, TDR, WHO/SPL: 17. Dennis
Degnan/Corbis: 11t. Eye of Science/SPL: 3cl, 25.
E. Guelio/CNRI/SPL: fr cover cl, b cover cr, 3tr,
23t. Dr. Chris Hale/SPL: 11b. Dr. P. Marazzi/SPL:
23. Matt Meadows, Peter Arnold Inc./SPL: 12.
Cordelia Molloy/SPL: 29. Alfred Pasieka/SPL: fr
cover tr, b cover tl, 2t, 16. Jose Luis Pelaez,
Inc./Corbis: 4t. Martin Reeves/Eye Ubiquitous: 22.
David Scarf/SPL: 18c. Ralf Schultheiss/Picture
Press/Corbis: 14. SPL: 19. Andrew Syred/SPL: fr
cover b, 3b, 10. Visioars/AKG London: 24.